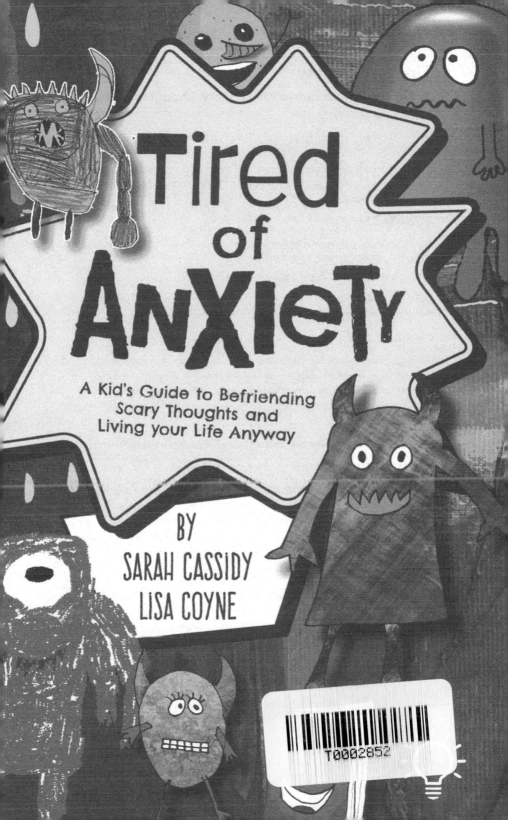

Tired
of
ANXIETY

A Kid's Guide to Befriending
Scary Thoughts and
Living your Life Anyway

BY
SARAH CASSIDY
LISA COYNE

T0002852

Tired of Anxiety

A Kid's Guide to Befriending Scary Thoughts and Living your Life Anyway

© Pavilion Publishing & Media

The authors have asserted their rights in accordance with the Copyright, Designs and Patents Act (1988) to be identified as the authors of this work.

Published by:

Pavilion Publishing and Media Ltd
Blue Sky Offices, 25 Cecil Pashley Way
Shoreham by Sea, West Sussex, BN43 5FF

Tel: 01273 434 943
Email: info@pavpub.com   Web: www.pavpub.com

Published 2022

A catalogue record for this book is available from the British Library.

ISBN: 978-1-80388-080-8

Pavilion Publishing and Media is a leading publisher of books, training materials and digital content in mental health, social care and allied fields. Pavilion and its imprints offer must-have knowledge and innovative learning solutions underpinned by sound research and professional values.

Authors: Sarah Cassidy and Lisa Coyne

Production and Content Coordinator: Hannah Hobbs, Pavilion Publishing and Media Ltd

Production editor: Mike Benge, Pavilion Publishing and Media Ltd

Cover design: Emma Dawe and Phil Morash, Pavilion Publishing and Media Ltd

Page layout and typesetting: Emma Dawe, Pavilion Publishing and Media Ltd

Printing: CMP

Contents

Special Thanks to Our Art Club Kids

This book would not have been possible without the many extraordinary kids that read all the versions of this book, gave us their opinions on every single chapter, and drew most of the artwork that you see. You all know who you are so we don't need to say your names, but we know you recognise your artwork. And much more than that, we recognise all the other work that you are doing and we are bowing deeply to you for that. We hope you keep it up. From the bottom of our hearts, we thank you for sharing your journeys with us and we sincerely hope you like the final book. It would not be this good without all of your expert advice along the way. This book is for you.

We'd also like to thank the staff and management at Louth Meath Education Training Board, who generously and graciously allowed us to use their space to host our art club each week. Without this, the club could not have safely taken place during COVID-19 and would have had to be cancelled.

Hello from Us

HI, I'M DR. SARAH and I live in Ireland with three kids, two dogs, one rabbit, three hens, two goldfish and one husband. I work with lots of kids who feel anxious and scared sometimes. I wrote this book because I feel anxious and scared sometimes too. I'm glad you're holding this book right now and I hope you keep reading.

HI, I'M DR. LISA and I not only help kids with their anxiety, but I've also worked through my own! I live near Boston with my family and three dogs – Doog, Lemon and Peach. My wish for you is that this book helps you know you are not alone, and helps you find your strengths – because they have been there all along.

Introduction for parents (or other trusted adults)

Dear parents,

Welcome to our book. This book is pitched at children who are anywhere between the ages of approximately 7 years old and 11 years old. If your child is a little younger or a little older, we still think they will learn from this book, but our examples will be pitched roughly within that age range.

We know, inside and out, that when you have an anxious child it can be really hard. Often, you don't know what to do, what to say, and whether it will help. It also can be heartbreaking and frustrating, in equal amounts, watching your child feel so fearful. You might worry that they are too vulnerable and will be hurt by the world if they don't sort this out. Or you might feel that there's no cause for them to be anxious, and that they just need to power through whatever the feared situation is. Sometimes parents feel that if their children experience too much anxiety, they will fall apart. And there are often real consequences of this for you and for the rest of your family. Often this disruption comes in the form of messed up routines, wobblers, meltdowns and an increase in the general stress and tension in the house for everyone else. Finally, lots of times parents can feel like it's their fault when these things happen.

We know.

We've been there too.

We understand.

We are here to help you find your way through this with our book. This book will provide evidence-based strategies for your child to create a different relationship with their anxiety. Instead of shutting down and opting out when they feel anxious, this book will encourage them to lean in, to face their fear, and explore it, expressly when *not* doing so prevents them from living a full, joyful, playful, and fun life. There are many books out there on child anxiety, but very few of them have been written in a style that kids really like, that resonates with their experiences, that they can understand and that are accessible to them.

This book was written for children with anxiety. The children that have already used the techniques in this book are real children with real anxiety from real families. They met in groups together. They practiced the skills together and they even created some of the art in this book based on their experiences.

But your child can't do this alone. They need you to help them walk through it. We know that some of your children will be strong readers and some will not. We know that some of your children will be very keen to read this book with you and some will initially take a little time to warm up to it. We know that some may prefer for you to read it to them and that some may prefer to read it to themselves. We also know for sure that all of them will have questions and will probably want to see what their parents think, and if their parents can help.

The good news is that how parents handle child anxiety can be a big piece of the puzzle. A parent's response to their child's anxiety can either help or hinder a child's progress when faced with that anxiety. The more you are willing to immerse yourself into the book with your child, and the more you reinforce the skills inside it – both by practicing yourself and noticing your child doing this – the better progress your child will make.

We know that most of you are probably not trained psychologists or teachers (though we certainly also welcome those of you that are), and are probably thinking, "I have no idea what to do or how to talk about this," or maybe, "I already know how to handle this. If I could just *do the thing* or if my child could just *do the thing*, then it would all be solved". So we've also written this book with the understanding that you, also, will learn as you go. And that's really important.

Although this book is written for your child, our intention was for you to read it *with* your child, and to learn alongside them. The best way for you to use it is to read a little bit every few days and make time and space to discuss it with your child. We encourage you to come with a beginner's mind, to be curious, to be open, to try out the things in the book yourself. We'll give you some tips in this chapter, and you can also refer to the companion book coming soon for parents called *Tired of Your Child's Anxiety?* for you to do a deeper dive into learning the skills that you will need going forward.

You may come to this book with preconceived notions about the best things to do when your child is anxious. Some of those ideas might be helpful, and some of them may not. Some of these ideas may come from what your parents or teachers taught you, and some of the ideas may come from what your neighbours, friends or colleagues think. You might also have lots of ideas that come out of popular culture and mass media. We encourage you to try to set aside those preconceived notions now as we are guessing that the fact that you are reading this book means that those things have probably not worked for you so far. So let the information in this book influence you now, also. Be curious about how the things you are doing to handle your child's anxiety *now* are working. Try the strategies we suggest for your child out for yourself. And model these strategies for your child. That is one of the most potent ways to teach and it will be the fastest way for your child to learn.

Here are some important rules of thumb for you as you work through the book with your child:

✔ Kids in this age group tend to learn less from what you *tell* them to do, and much more from what you *show* them to do. How you as a parent handle your own anxiety is really important.

✔ Although you may be feeling that you should protect your child from feeling anxiety at all costs, sometimes that takes away opportunities for your child to learn that anxiety can't actually hurt them.

✔ You might, on the other hand, feel like you should push your child – just make them get through it, so they will toughen up. And while that might be a useful once-in-a-while short term strategy, it doesn't really help them learn to change their relationship with their anxiety. They will simply learn to bottle it up or white knuckle it and "get through it" meanwhile it will stay the big monster it has always been.

✔ Help your child to face their fears gradually. That's the best way to help your child move forward and it's the way that has the strongest evidence base.

What will help you on this journey also includes the following:

1. Empathy – help your child feel that you understand how they are feeling. Some tips for how to do that include; listening, reflecting what they say, and touching the part inside you that might know what that feels like.

2. Share – maybe share a story (at the right time) about your own anxiety. This will help to make a safe space for your child to talk about their anxiety because they know that you've been there too.

3. Model – lean into your own fears and discomforts to show your child how to do the same.

4. Resist trying to protect them from feeling anxiety (except when they are truly in an unsafe situation) and encourage them to lean into their discomfort.

5. Be flexible – this will not be a straight path and there are no magic bullets. Give your child time, invite, collaborate, help them choose to face their fears. Resist being coercive or punishing them when they don't choose to face their fears.

6. Block avoidance – having trouble going to school? Go anyway. Avoidance feeds anxiety – so shaping bravery by doing things even when children feel doubtful or scared helps.

7. Be systematic – read the book in small doses appropriate to your child's developmental level, and keep at it. Think of it the way you would think about taking antibiotics – they don't work if you take them only once in a while. Moreover, taking antibiotics only occasionally and not at the correct dosage can actually make things much worse by making the infection resistant to antibiotics! The same thing happens to avoidance when your child is anxious. The more consistent you are in the practice of reading bits of the book and facing fears and really making it into a family practice,

the faster things will go. But if you're inconsistent, you might end up creating an even bigger, nastier, scarier version of the anxiety monster.

8. Measure success in small steps, and don't forget to reinforce each of those steps. They may seem small to you, but they might feel monumental to your child.

9. Make a space to feel your own anxiety. If you have a child unwilling to feel anxiety, it's very likely that there's a parent feeling the same way. Work on facing your own fears as you go and do it as a team with your child.

10. Be gentle with yourself. You won't do this right all the time either. You're human. We understand. We've been there too and there are days when we do all the 'right' things and days when we don't. That's completely normal and just part of what being human is. And when we have a day, or an hour or a minute that didn't go how we imagined it would, we can always pick ourselves up, dust ourselves off and try again. We're with you, in the background, cheering for you too.

1:

Getting to know your anxiety

Have you ever felt really scared, but you weren't sure why? Like, maybe you had butterflies in your stomach, or maybe you were worried about bad stuff that might happen, but you weren't even sure what that bad stuff might be. Maybe you started to get a pain in your head from thinking so much about it. Or you started to feel dizzy or weak or sweaty or all clenched up.

Were you ever trying to do something completely normal but your mind just wouldn't let you? Like, for example, were you ever trying to join a new football team but your mind kept telling you that you'd trip over your own feet or that you were rubbish at football and that everyone would laugh at you? Did you ever want to go to the zoo, but your mind told you that a lion or a bear might break out of their cage and gobble you up?

Were you ever trying to go to sleep but your mind just wouldn't stop worrying? Or maybe it told you that there were horrible scary monsters under your bed that were going to take you away somewhere? Or maybe your parents were trying to get you to eat your dinner, but you were afraid that you might vomit, and that would be *terrifying*?

If these things happen to you, then you might have a little thing called anxiety. Of course, if it's happening to you, it probably doesn't feel very little. In fact, it probably feels like **the biggest thing in the entire world!**

Well, we've got some good news and some bad news. The good news is that **everybody** has anxiety! And there's a good reason for that. Imagine for a moment that you never ever felt anxious or scared. Great, right? Unless there was a wild rhinoceros running straight at you! How would you know that you should get out of the way and FAST? You see, anxiety is *information*: it is our body's way of helping us to stay safe. We need it, and it can be helpful... sometimes. The problem is that sometimes our mind thinks we should be on the lookout for danger *all of the time* (even when there are NO wild rhinos running straight at us).

If you are like most people, you probably do your best to avoid feeling anxious in any number of ways, like:

- avoiding the things that makes you anxious, or

- asking someone else, like one of your parents, to make you feel better, or

- hiding that you feel anxious, or

- trying to somehow block out that anxious feeling by distracting yourself with a video game, or

- by just staying really, really close to your parents or siblings or friends so that you feel just a bit safer,

  for a while,

  when they are there with you, maybe...

But here's the thing about anxiety. It's sort of like a growly annoying little pesky monster – and each time it growls, you do something to avoid it because of course that growling is actually quite scary. And feeding the monster works for a bit and maybe then for another while. Until suddenly it doesn't work anymore... and the whole thing starts to backfire.

Because each time you try to avoid it, you are basically feeding it little treats to keep it quiet for a while. And after it gets a lot of these little treats – because you keep feeding it – it can grow pretty big...

and you may find that what started as a little niggling worry or fear has now grown into something enormous and you have now backed yourself into a corner.

The corner you find yourself in might not feel very safe anymore....

and you might not know what to do…

because maybe all the stuff you've tried so far (the treats you've been throwing to the growly annoying anxiety monster to keep it quiet) isn't working so well anymore…

and by now you are probably feeling really STUCK because all the things you usually do to stop your anxiety just don't work forever and in fact, you're all out of ideas.

And you're probably absolutely exhausted too.

So now what?

Well, what if we tried something different, just for a moment? What if, instead of running a thousand miles an hour away from anxiety, you stopped, took a breath, and actually got a bit curious about anxiety? Imagine you just found something cool in the bottom of a box in your garage or in your attic. And you opened it up and took a closer look and said to yourself, "Hey what is this thing anyway?"

Will you try this with us? We're just going to ask a few questions because we're really curious what this might be like for you.

When your anxiety visits you …

What is it like?

What do you notice about it?

Where does it live in your body?

When anxiety is around, what does your body do?

Take a moment to answer these questions, either out loud with your parent, or just quietly to yourself.

When you think about your anxiety, or when it visits you (totally uninvited we're sure!!), does it feel like you are in charge? Or is it in charge? Who feels bigger – you, or it? See if you can draw a picture of you and your anxiety below.

Who's Bigger – Me or My Anxiety?

When your anxiety visits and feels pretty big, you might notice that...

...you have all sorts of feelings in your body, and

...you have all sorts of emotions in your heart, and

...you have all sorts of thoughts running through your mind.

While everyone has anxiety, the experience of anxiety can be quite different for each person. So we'd love to take a little time to write or draw what this might be like for you in your body, in your heart, and in your mind when your anxiety comes for a visit. What do YOU feel like when anxiety happens? Can you tell us about that? For example, some people get a pain in their head. Some people feel sad about being anxious. Some people think, "I really wish I could make these scary thoughts go away!" Some people find it really hard to put things into words. If that's true for you, we've made a place for you to write or draw what it's like for you when anxiety visits below.

When Anxiety Visits... Things I feel in my body

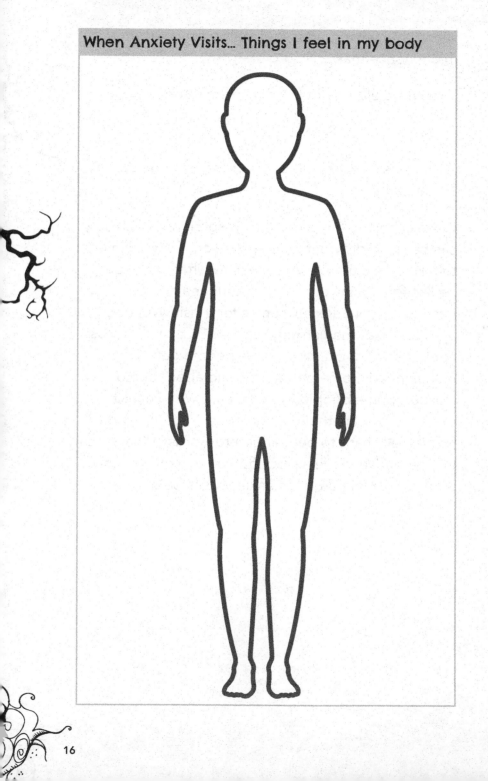

Things I feel in my heart

Thoughts that my mind tells me

Or here's another idea you can try.

If you imagined your anxiety like... a cartoon character you could draw, what would it look like? Sound like? Feel Like? Maybe you can even imagine what it might smell and taste like!

We invite you to take a little time, and write or draw what your anxiety looks like in the space below. If we were drawing ours, it would be a big bossy person, giving us advice ALL OF THE TIME, whether we liked it or not! Or maybe it would be a television or radio with the volume on so high that we cannot think straight. If yours was a cartoon character, what would yours look like? What would it say to you? If you could name it, what would you call it? (Just for fun, we call ours Frank and Frank is sooooo ridiculously bossy and he thinks he knows everything and he usually has one hand on his hip and the other one is pointing a finger at us. Ouch – that feels uncomfortable even as we write about it.). See if you can draw your anxiety in the space below and while you're at it, give it a name.

My Anxiety: What I'd call it:

_____

Introducing Mindfulness

Oh good! You're still here!

Guess what? While you were drawing/colouring/describing you and your anxiety, you have been practicing a new skill that we call mindfulness! And here is the recipe for being mindful:

- slowing down

- getting curious

- noticing, on purpose

Notice how you are feeling right now. Let's take a few moments to check in with ourselves. What did you notice about your anxiety when you were drawing, reading, writing about it? What was it like to learn that you are separate from your anxiety? You're the person doing the drawing and writing about the anxiety. You are not the same as your anxiety. In fact, what is it like to hear that there's a lot more to you than just your anxiety?

Mindfulness is like finding a quiet place where you can stop running so hard away from your anxiety. It might even become a place where you can get to know your anxiety... and maybe even become friends with your anxiety.

Wait a minute, what did they say?

There are a lot of different ways to be mindful. Here are some ideas that you can try out. Remember the steps: slow down, get curious, and notice on purpose:

- ✔ 5 things that you hear in the world around you right now

- ✔ if you are eating, notice what the food tastes like

- ✔ 5 parts of your body and how those parts feel (you can tense your muscles and then let them go loose and see what that's like!)

- ✔ what it feels like to breathe in and breathe out

- ✔ 5 things you can touch in the room around you

- ✔ 5 things your mind is saying to you right now

Here is a cool thing to try out, if you like. Do you feel ok to close your eyes? If so, you can have someone you trust reading this next piece to you. Or you can listen to Dr. Sarah reading it by downloading the recording from the website that we include under the title of each audio track (www.pavpub.com/tired-of-anxiety-resources). Or if you're by yourself and you can't listen to the recording, you can read through the piece and then close your eyes and try to go through what you've just read quietly in your mind.

Audio track

www.pavpub.com/tired-of-anxiety-resources

First, find a quiet spot. Get yourself settled and comfy on a chair, and hold yourself upright but not overly rigid. Just make sure that you can breathe in and out comfortably.

Hold your hands loosely in your lap, or by your sides. Close your eyes if you feel ok to do that, and just breathe.

Next, remember our steps: slow down, get curious, and notice on purpose.

Start by noticing your breathing. Take your time.

What is it like right now? Is your breathing fast or slow? Are you taking deep breaths or shallow breaths?

You don't have to do anything different.

Just notice where your body is at, right here, in this moment.

Our breath is like an anchor because it is always with us. It has never forgotten us, and nobody ever had to teach us how to breathe. Our bodies always knew how to do this thing called breathing. Isn't that amazing? Nobody ever had to teach us how. So just take a few moments to breathe, in and out. In and out, in and out. Like you always do.

You might notice that as you're breathing and really focusing on it, sometimes your breath will slow down all by itself and your breaths will get deeper.

Is there anything else that you notice right now?

We've been talking and thinking about some stuff that might be difficult for you and sometimes that can affect our bodies too. Do you notice anything in particular? Do you have any tension, or stress or strain, or tightness anywhere in your body? Or can you notice any different kinds of feelings? Tinglyness? Numbness? Hotness? Coldness? It's ok if you do, and its ok if you don't. All we want you to do right now is to take a few moments to notice what is happening in your body. Check in with you.

How are you doing?

And how about your mind? Is it buzzing about or is it still? And what can you notice about your thoughts? Did your thoughts carry you away or did they slow down while you were paying attention to your breath? Are they fast or slow or somewhere in between? Again, you don't have to do anything different at all. Just notice what your mind is doing or saying right now. Get curious about what your mind is telling you for the next few moments. Really checking in with you.

You see, any time you are noticing your breath, you might also notice:

- feelings in your body

- emotions in your heart

- thoughts in your mind...

...and maybe all three at the same time, all jumbled up! And that's ok! You're doing a great job practicing mindfulness. It can be fun... it can be easy... it can be messy... it can be confusing. For some people it can be peaceful... or it can be weird. Just remember the three ingredients – slowing down, being curious and noticing on purpose.

Good. Very good. You did it. Nice job. You're very welcome here – and believe it or not, so is your anxiety. And we are so glad you came.

And when you're ready – and there's absolutely no rush – slowly start to notice your body in the chair again, your feet on the floor. Any noises in the room, any smells in the room, and slowly open up your eyes and come back fully to the room. And have a good stretch.

How was it? What did you think?

Home practice

(What?? Did you say homework??! Yep, we sure did, but it might even be fun. Let's check it out.)

Across the next week, see if you can practice your noticing skills. Take five minutes every day and just notice, on purpose, what feelings are in your body, what emotions are in your heart and what thoughts are in your mind. You don't need to do anything other than notice. It might seem weird at first, but the more you practice noticing things on purpose, the easier it will get.

Our brains as threat detectors

In the last chapter we talked about anxiety, why we need it, and how to stop feeding it by practicing mindfulness. And when we say 'mindfulness' all we mean is slowing down, being curious, and noticing on purpose what is around us and how we are feeling.

One of the things that we can notice is how our mind talks to us when we are feeling anxious. You remember, in the first chapter, how we talked about why we *need* anxiety? And that anxiety is *information*? Well, our mind – the part of our brain that talks to us (gives us advice) – has an important job when it comes to anxiety: to tell us how we should understand things so that we are safe.

You see, our mind is basically this amazing threat-detecting machine. It helps us to navigate the world. And if we think about it, our ancestors lived in a world that was a lot more dangerous than the world we live in today...

Our ancestors didn't have the same types of houses that could shelter them from the cold or heat or wild storms and winds...

And there would have been a *lot* of wild animals roaming about the place...

So they were in danger a lot of the time. They needed to have a threat detector that was wide awake ALL OF THE TIME. We modern humans have inherited that exact same mind that our ancestors had. On top of that, our mind is super-careful to let us know what we should avoid! And we modern humans have kept this fantastic threat detecting machine because it helps to keep us safe from danger. I mean it's better to be safe than sorry, right? Especially when there might be wild rhinos running around!

So, when your mind detects a threat, it is actually just doing its job. It is not trying to make you upset or scared or trying to ruin your day and it's definitely not trying to stop you from going to sleep at night.

And it turns out that there are even parts of your brain that are especially good at detecting threats. For example, there's this tiny little guy, called an amygdala, and this little guy is AMAZING at detecting all sorts of threats. You wouldn't believe that such a tiny little thing could have such an important job, but it does. You don't need to remember what that little guy is called, but we do want you to remember that this is kind of like your brain's alarm system.

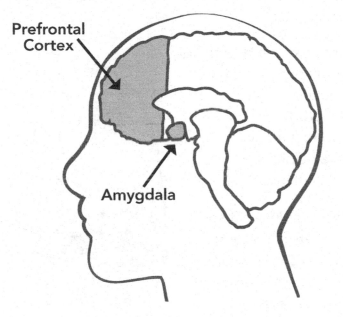

Prefrontal Cortex

Amygdala

When something starts to signal danger, the amygdala goes on high alert so that you can fight something dangerous, run away from something dangerous, or roll over and play dead if that would be more useful in that moment. You've probably heard of 'fight or flight' before. Well, when your body goes into fight or flight mode, it also stops thinking and reasoning so that it can put all of its energy into fighting or getting away. In order to do that quickly, when the alarm system gets triggered, the part of your brain that does the thinking and reasoning (the pre-frontal cortex or PFC) actually goes offline. In other words, the part of your brain that makes you think and make reasonable decisions has switched off completely. So you're not thinking and reasoning anymore. Instead, you are just responding to the alarm signal.

But one of the best things about your mind's threat detecting ability can also be a problem... our mind isn't always 100% helpful (even when it thinks it is!).

For example, what sorts of threats or dangers or worries does your mind detect? See if you can slow down, get curious, and notice on purpose, just for a few moments, whatever scary or worrisome thoughts your mind is telling you. Write or draw in the space below what your mind tells you to be on alert for.

My Anxious Mind: A Threat Detecting Machine

Part of what is tough about your mind being really good at detecting threats (although sometimes also unhelpful) is that it's often hard to tell *when* to listen to it, and when *not* to. I mean, you can't turn it off, right?

You see, your threat detecting mind is really super useful if you are actually running away from a rhino, but what if there's no rhino here and you've accidentally turned off the thinking and reasoning parts of your brain?? What if your amygdala is like a super sensitive smoke alarm in your house? Now if there was actually a fire, you would definitely want that smoke detector turned on full blast.

my house

But did it ever happen that your real-life smoke detector went off and you thought, "Oh no! There's a fire! Run!" But when you went downstairs you found out that your Dad had just accidentally burned some brownies? And while you were disappointed that there weren't any brownies (we'd be disappointed too!), you also realised that there was no particular reason to run out of the house right now.

Not again, Dad!!

You see sometimes your threat-detecting brain doesn't exactly have all the information it needs. It is so busy shining the light on the danger in a situation that it might miss some other really key information. You see, burning some brownies does not require you to run from the house screaming with a little brother on one hip and a favourite toy on the other one. (Ok a few quiet tears over the burned brownies would be completely understandable. We love brownies too.) But what other information might you be missing here if you go running out of the house every time someone burns some brownies? Let's slow it down a bit.

Here's one place where mindfulness can be super helpful. Remember the three steps? They were:

 slow down

 get curious

 notice, on purpose

And we are going to add one more step to those that will help with that pesky threat-detecting mind:

 step back from our thoughts

But how exactly do you do that?

One way to do that is to notice that you can *choose* to listen to what your mind tells you... or you could observe what's going on with your five senses: touch, sight, hearing, tasting, even smelling! Here's how:

What if, instead of running out the door every time an alarm went off, maybe you could try checking out some other information that might be here as well. Shine the light of your attention around the room to see a bit better what might be happening.

You might hear your mind's threat detector and of course you would listen to it, the same way you would listen to a fire alarm if you heard one! But let's imagine for a second that you can also have a look around and see what else is happening here.

You see, if you slow down, get curious, notice on purpose, and *step back from your thoughts*, it gives you a chance to use the other parts of your brain too. If you slow things down, you can look around and decide whether or not you're actually in danger. If you're actually in danger, then ok, you should run for it. But we'd be willing to bet that there are at least a few situations where people are running for the hills before they've even checked in with what else is happening here. The reason we know this is because we do this too. And believe us when we tell you that it takes a lot of practice to slow down this wonderful threat-detecting machine we all have. But if you slow it down, you get to use the thinking and reasoning parts of your brain as well. These can help you to make more thoughtful decisions about what your next best move in each situation might be.

Let's take a moment to check in with your anxiety, and see the kinds of things that your mind might say when you are feeling scared. See if you can step back from your thoughts and see if your mind, the threat detector, went off and there wasn't actually any fire or rhinos. Write or draw about some of those times here.

My Anxious Mind: False Alarms

The Beginner's Guide to Your Own Mind: Threat Detection 101

Now we are going to ask you a funny question: where are you right now? I mean, we know you are *here*, at least your *body* is here – but where is your mind? Is it worrying about stuff that might happen in the future? Or is it maybe thinking about stuff that happened in the past? Or maybe it is going back and forth between both of those times?

If you notice this, then you have just discovered one of your mind's coolest perks: it can *time travel*! When you are anxious, this is one of the ways your mind keeps its eyes on potential dangers – looking out for what might be ahead, and keeping a close eye on stuff that might sneak up in the rearview mirror – like mistakes from the past. Sometimes this is helpful and sometimes it is not.

Try this: see if you can write down or draw some of the places your mind goes when it travels to the past and when it travels to the future.

Places from the past your mind goes to	Places in the future your mind goes to

In order to start learning whether it's helpful or not for your mind to time travel, you can anchor yourself where you are, right now. And the good news is you already know how to do that! All you have to do is the four steps of slowing down, getting curious, noticing on purpose, and stepping back from your thoughts. If you like, you can go ahead and try this now...

You see, it turns out that your mind does a lot of cool stuff that helps with threat detection. Let's take it for a test drive and see what you notice.

See what happens when you read these phrases below:

Mary had a little…

Jack and Jill went up the…

Twinkle twinkle little…

Now try this!

I'm a good…

I'm a bad…

Anxiety is…

Did you notice that your mind fills in the blanks? And did you notice how fast that happened, without you even trying? We think it's pretty cool how minds do that. Your mind is so *fast*, and thoughts can pop up so quickly.

Try this next thing: Slow down, close your eyes and imagine… a slice of lemon… imagine what it smells like… what it feels like in your hand… its colour… its bumpy skin… and now imagine chomping down on it so the juice squirts into your mouth….

Now think about your favourite sweet. Slow down, close your eyes and imagine what it looks like... if you are holding it in your hand... whether it has a smell... and now, taking a big bite (or a lick – whatever works) of your favourite sweet.

With the lemon, did you notice squishing up your face? With your favourite sweet, did you notice your mouth watering a bit? Did you get a little hungry? Even though there are no *actual* lemons here, and no sweets either. That's because your mind can't always tell the difference between a *thought* and the real thing. That's a little crazy, right?

This is important to notice when it comes to anxiety... what it means is that your mind has a hard time telling the difference between real rhinoceroses and the ones you might be imagining with your thoughts... think a minute – has your mind ever told you to be scared of something that, once you tried it, wasn't so scary? Or maybe even was actually fun?

Now one last thing before we move on.

You know that thing you do when your threat detector goes off? Does it work for you? I mean does it reeaaaallllly work for you? If so, you can close this book right now and never pick it up again unless you're super bored and can't think of another single, solitary thing to do with your valuable time. But if not, read on because we think we've got some interesting things to tell you.

What do you do when your threat detector goes off?

Write or draw about that here.

What I Do When My Threat Detector Goes Off

Hey, look at you, you've done a great job getting to know your threat detector! And you learned it by practicing the mindfulness skills in Chapter 1 and adding the skill of stepping back from your thoughts. Well done! Right now though, you are probably wondering what to do about all of that, since you may have noticed that some of the stuff you do when your threat detector goes off doesn't actually work that well. If you are curious about what you might do differently, read on.

 # Home practice

For this week, we'd like you to just practice your noticing skills some more. When you notice that your threat detector goes off, see if you can slow down, get curious, and notice on purpose what is happening in your mind, heart and body. Once you have noticed those things, see if you can step back from what you've noticed and just observe that you are able to do that – to step back. The more you practice stepping back from your thoughts, feelings and actions, the easier it gets to do those things.

3:

More on mindfulness

We hear a lot about mindfulness these days and we think that's great that so many people know about it now. But what we are interested in learning now is what do you think mindfulness is?

Can you tell us what you think mindfulness is in the space below?

Well, guess what, we've been doing lots of it already when we were doing our noticing exercises. Really, it's pretty straightforward like we've talked about before. It just means paying attention, on purpose, to what is happening in this moment right now.

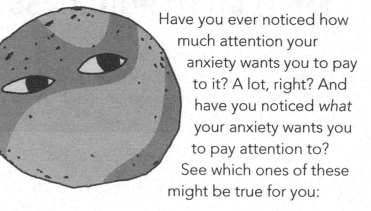

Have you ever noticed how much attention your anxiety wants you to pay to it? A lot, right? And have you noticed *what* your anxiety wants you to pay attention to? See which ones of these might be true for you:

Your anxiety might want you to pay attention to:

- scary stuff that might happen in the future

- mistakes you made in the past

- worries about how to handle scary situations in the future

- feeling like you might get left out

- remembering times you were lonely

- stuff you are afraid of at bedtime

Have you noticed that all of these are things that are either in the future or the past? In this way, anxiety makes it hard to be here, right now!

Have you noticed that anxiety is a pretty good storyteller, but its stories are always about bad stuff

that might happen, or scary stuff you should avoid?
This is one of the ways that it tries to keep your
attention on it alone – and focused on the "what ifs"
and "might happens" rather than the present.

Take some time here to draw the things that anxiety
wants you to pay attention to.

So how do you learn to let anxiety talk away at you,
and pay attention to other things too? By practicing
mindfulness – paying attention to the here and now.
And there are tons of ways to practice that! You don't
have to sit cross legged on a cushion, with your eyes
closed, saying "Ohhhmm" to do mindfulness.

You can even do mindfulness while you are doing everyday tasks like washing your hands. To do this, you could start by noticing the temperature of the water as it comes out of the tap. Notice how it feels on your skin as you place your hands under the spray of water, and maybe you can feel the slippery sensation of the soap on your hands, and maybe the soap has a certain smell. Can you breathe that in?? Really notice it. What does it smell like? Is it a strong smell? Does the smell fade as you rinse the soap off your hands? Did the soap make bubbles? What did the water look like going down the drain? Did it splatter and make different patterns or rivulets or did it go straight down? What do your hands feel like now? Can you notice the water dripping off them? What about as you dry your hands? Do they feel different now? Can you still smell the soap? If you have a sink nearby, you can put this workbook aside right now and try this activity.

You can also do mindfulness by just paying attention to your breath. You don't need any special training for this or any special equipment because your breath is always with you. Let's do that right now, just for a few moments.

Pause, observe the breath coming in through your nose. Is it warm or cool? How many seconds can you inhale for? Now breathe out through your mouth. Is the air different? Was it warmer coming out than it was going in? Can you notice the air filling up your lungs? What would it feel like if you held your breath for a few seconds? I bet it's a relief to then let it go. Your breath is always with you. It's like an anchor. What happens to your chest when you breathe in and out? What happens to your stomach? Do they go up and down and in and out? What happens when you really focus on your breathing?

For us, we think focusing on our breathing or really doing any mindfulness practice tends to slow everything down. This helps us to stay in *this* present moment rather than running at 100 miles an hour trying to run away from stuff our mind tells us might hurt us. You see, being mindful encourages us to pause often and to see what is REALLY happening in a situation, instead of our minds going into over-drive and telling us the *worst possible thing that could happen* (AGGGHHHHHH DISASTER ZONE!!). Being mindful helps us to pause on that and simply be here.

Oh that's nice. I like that.

And here's another nice surprise for you – guess what else you've been doing when you've been doing mindful noticing and deep breathing? You've actually been turning down the volume on your amygdala (remember, the alarm system in your brain?) and turning back on your thinking and reasoning brain. So while you can't get rid of your amygdala because you need it, you can turn your attention to something else that makes more sense in a moment. Wow! You're magnificent! Isn't that amazing!? You get to be in charge of where you put your attention.

What other mindfulness activities can you think of??

Here are some that we like: dancing, singing, baking, playing sports, gardening, listening to music, doing yoga, even brushing your teeth or eating your breakfast. But the trick is that whatever activity you choose, do it with your *full attention*. So if you are baking but thinking about a test at school (and we do that too, so no big deal if it happens), just gently return your attention to the feel of the dough that you are kneading with your fingers, or the smell of the chocolate chips or any information that you can take in with your five senses while you do the activity.

Can you try some of these at home? With your parents or your siblings or maybe with your friends or with a teacher??

You can pretty much build mindfulness into any activity because if you are being mindful, it just means that you are paying attention to all the sensory information that you are receiving from the activity. And mindfulness doesn't have to be slow and sitting or lying down. You can be mindfully dancing by really paying attention to the way it feels when your body moves a certain way or the sound your shoes make when they move across the floor or by paying really close attention to the music you are dancing to, and by paying attention to the drums or the beat or the rhythm, whatever works for you.

But the more you pay attention, on purpose, to this present moment, the better you'll be at mindfulness. And that means that your mind doesn't get to run away on you and make you think and feel like everything is an ABSOLUTE DISASTER at the loudest volume imaginable! That means when Frank (or whatever you call your mind) pipes up, you can pause for a

second and decide what you want to do next. And the more you get practiced at slowing things down and noticing what is actually happening, instead of running a million miles quickly in the other direction, the easier it gets to pause for a moment, notice what is happening and choose how *you* want to go forward.

You might have questions about what to do with anxiety while you are practicing mindfulness. And the answer is... nothing!

You don't have to do one thing about it. You can let it be there, and notice it trying to pull you into the future or the past, and choose to be in the present anyway, without doing what it says. It takes practice, so try it and see what happens!

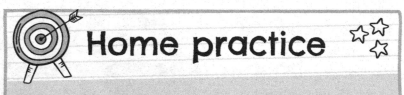

Home practice

Choose any mindfulness practice that you like and do it a few times this week. That's all. But jot it down here and also write down how it worked for you so that we can remember later which ones work best for you.

4:

Control and avoidance

Ok, back to what works and what doesn't. You see, here's the thing. When things feel scary or dangerous to us, most people want to avoid them. This is how people try to control things in their lives that feel scary or dangerous. And of course, it's perfectly normal that you would want to try to fix those feelings or make something dangerous go away or somehow not be dangerous any more. When that happens you're just reacting to a threat that your system has detected. And if there is a threat to the system, then you need to keep your system safe. Simple. But if all you're doing is keeping your system safe all the time, is there a chance that you might be missing something important?

Let's think about anxiety and worry thoughts again. What lots of people do with anxiety is they try to control it. For example, imagine you are a kid who struggles to read. You probably get really nervous every time you pick up a book. And you might have thoughts like, *I am*

terrible at reading. I am so bad. I'll never be good at it and people at school will laugh at me and think I'm stupid. And those thoughts *hurt*. So then you put the book down. Bye bye, anxiety! See you later, hurt!

And that might work really well... for the time being. It's just that, if you put that book down every time you are supposed to be reading... it doesn't really ever make reading any easier. Your reading never gets any better because you get so worked up every time you try to read that you feel like you just can't do it. So your reading never gets any better.

As a matter of fact, avoiding it might even make it worse. Your teachers might get annoyed because they think you don't care. Your parents might get annoyed because they think you're not trying. And because you're not getting any reading practice, the days and books might pile up... and that mountain of unread books might feel more and more overwhelming..

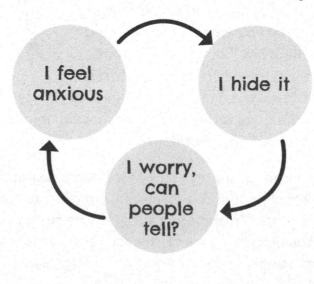

Now not only are you worried about your anxiety, you're also worried about whether people can tell, and you're even *more* scared about feeling anxious again, and you try even *harder* to hide it! And it starts to feel like a snowball rolling down a hill, gathering more worries, and more anxiety as it goes. By the time it gets to the bottom of the hill, it has turned into an enormous avalanche and has taken out some villages and children in its path.

But the thing is, maybe you really and truly want to do your best. Maybe you really want your parents to be proud of you. Maybe you want your teacher to know that you want to do your best. You even might sometimes be interested in some of the books that you see your friends reading.

Running away from things that are hard might make sense... at first. But the bad news is that it never makes that stuff get any easier. And just as we discussed in Chapter 2, it would make sense if the stuff we were running from was an actual rhinoceros. But most of the time, there are no rhinos around here. There are just threat detectors telling you to run away because they are only focusing on threat, and not noticing that you are not *actually* in physical danger.

Here's a crazy idea: What do you think would happen if instead of running away from the stuff that was scary, we ran towards the things that mattered most to us? Instead of avoiding, what if we tried our four steps:

✔ Slow down

✔ Get curious

✔ Notice on purpose

✔ Step back from your thoughts...

...and added one more step? Here it is:

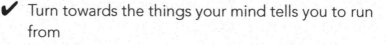

✔ Turn towards the things your mind tells you to run from

Try that idea on for size!

But first, let's slow this down a bit, shall we?

You might be asking yourself, why on earth would you do a crazy thing like that? Well, let's see.

Are there things you miss doing that your struggle with anxiety has taken away from you? Are there things you wish you could do but then anxiety pops up and your mind says, *Not a chance!* We are guessing that maybe there are. Something brought you or your parents or teachers to buy this book for you, right?

See if you can draw or write down some things that you might do if you weren't avoiding all the things your threat detector was getting triggered by.

Learning how to turn towards the scary stuff takes a little time. It's helpful to practice your four steps.

When you slow down, get curious, and notice on purpose... how does that make you feel? What does your heart need right now? See if you can get really quiet and listen in. People often ask you what you're thinking and that's a valid question too, but see if you can step back from your thoughts. What we really want to know is how you feel. And you can't tell how you feel... unless you slow down enough to actually take a look.

When you have spent a long time running away from feeling anxious, you may have also run very far from the things you most care about. And you can feel really *stuck* or trapped. On one hand, when anxiety shows up, and your mind gets loud, you might want to run in the other direction. And yet, if you try to take a step towards the stuff you care about, that pesky anxiety gets in your way. You see, when you walk towards the stuff that is important to you, it's perfectly normal that anxiety and doubt might show up.

Can you step inside that stuck space for a while? Breathe your way into it?

When you want something that isn't here right now, it hurts, doesn't it? When you don't get to see your friends, you might feel lonely and sad. And when you keep running from anxiety and it keeps coming back, it might feel like there is something really, really wrong, like there's something broken and you just don't know how to fix it. And when this happens, it might feel like your heart is actually broken.

If you are willing, take a few moments to write or draw or colour what it is like for you in your stuck space. If it's hard to put this into words, see if these questions might help. See if you can feel your stuck space. If you could imagine it as an object, would it be:

- rough, or smooth?

- big or small?

- a deep dark hole that you accidentally fell into, and now you don't know how to get out of?

- something with edges, or not?

- sharp or dull?

- heavy or light?

- solid like a rock, or fluid like water?

- a bright or dark colour?

- smaller than you, or bigger?

- flat like a blanket, or round like a ball?

- still or wriggly?

What did you notice about slowing down, getting curious, and noticing your anxiety on purpose? What is different about going towards it and examining it rather than running away from it? What did you learn? Did anything surprise you? Was there anything that happened that you didn't expect?

It's important to know that whatever you're feeling right now is ok. There are no right or wrong answers or feelings here. We just want you to notice this feeling and let it in. This feeling didn't do anything wrong and we're not going to push it away.

We're not saying that you have to like it, or want it. We are encouraging you to listen to it, to see what it has to say.

Here's a curious thing, it turns out that if you make space for these difficult thoughts and feelings and actually let them in and have a look at them, you can actually learn some really important things about yourself.

What if this feeling could be telling you something that is really important? Listen for a moment. What if when you run away from difficult feelings, you might be missing something really valuable?

Sometimes the biggest, scariest feelings you have are the ones that help you to discover the things you care the most about.

You might learn that you don't have to stop your thoughts and feelings or cover them up or pretend they are not there. Sometimes it is helpful to slow it all down so that you get a chance to look properly at what information your head, heart and body are telling you right now. You can listen to what both your hearts and your minds are saying and you can then decide how you choose to go forward.

Let's do that right now. Listen for a moment to what is in your heart. If you like, you can have someone you trust read this next short section to you. Or you can listen to Dr. Sarah's recording. Or else, read it quietly to yourself and then close your eyes and try to think back on the questions asked.

Audio track

www.pavpub.com/tired-of-anxiety-resources

Getting yourself settled into your chair again, closing over your eyes again if this feels comfortable for you.

How would you like to go forward? What do you want to move towards in your life?

Think about the stuff that your struggle with scary thoughts and feelings has taken away. What do you want back?

What does your heart say about that? Let's unpack this idea too. Just like you might unpack a suitcase. What's in that suitcase? Take a few minutes now and listen to what your heart is saying. What does your heart want most? Remember it's ok for your heart to ask for whatever that is.

And now breathe into whatever it is your heart is asking for. As though the very act of listening to your heart and breathing into what it asks for can somehow make it real. Take a few minutes and imagine listening to your heart and breathing in and out. And each thing that your heart wants. See if you can really imagine it now. Every little detail. See if you can see yourself doing whatever it is your heart really wants. Whatever it is.

Remember that this is your imagination, so go ahead and think big. The usual rules don't apply here. We're not asking you to think about what's possible, we're asking you what your heart wants. See if you can see yourself not being scared, or being scared but doing what's important anyway, or sleeping alone or having lots of friends, or having more quiet time to yourself, or reading really well.

And whatever it is that your heart wants, just breathe it in. A few more times now. That's it. Keep going. Breathe in and out, in and out. In and out.

Then slowly, and when you're ready – because there is no rush – slowly start to bring yourself back to the room you're sitting in. Notice the chair that holds you. Notice the floor that's below you. Notice any smells that are in the room. Notice the temperature of the air.

And finally, open over your eyes and have a good stretch and come back fully to the room. What was that like?

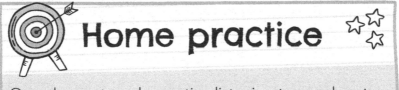

Home practice

Over the next week, practice listening to your heart. You don't have to do anything at all with what your heart says. Just listen to what it asks for. And breathe, again and again, breathe, while listening to what your heart wants.

5:

Values – what you care about

Imagine that you are going to go on a trip all by yourself, someplace that you have never been before – and it is actually to another planet! And let's say that when you leave to go to this planet, it's sooo far away that you probably wouldn't be able to come home for many years. The rocket ship flight crew tell you that you can bring with you *only one suitcase*. Imagine that once you get there, you will have the basic stuff you need, like food and water, and a room and a bed and clothes and toys and things. So no need to pack those things.

Imagine that you are in your house, in your room, and in front of you is an empty suitcase. You can only put five things in it to take with you to the new planet. These five things should help you keep those things that are most important to you in your heart as you travel to your new world. Take some time to think about what you would put in your suitcase. Write down or draw those things that you would want in your suitcase.

Things for my suitcase:

Lots of times when you get stuck struggling with anxiety, you can lose touch with the stuff that is really important to you – the stuff you keep in your heart. This is why it might be helpful to think about what you would put in your suitcase.

We call those things that are really important to us *values*. Values are not "things" that you can have.

They are not goals either. So if you really wanted a puppy, that's great and we love puppies too, but that's a *goal*. And once you get that puppy – *if* you get that puppy – you've reached your goal. Values are somewhat different to goals. They are the things we care about that make us who we are.

Take a moment to think about a superhero or maybe someone famous that you really look up to – maybe even someone in your family. Think about what you think is cool, or what you admire about that person. What is it?

A few years ago, I met two of the *coolest people* ever. I was eating lunch at a restaurant, and there were two guys in blue jumpsuits with lots of badges all over them. They were ASTRONAUTS! And they had just returned from a long trip on the international space station! What I found so cool about them was that they were *explorers*. And only a very few people on Earth have ever done what they did – hang out in space!

I realized that something really important to me – one of my values – is *exploring and discovering new things!*

Take a few moments and have a think about someone you really love, or someone you really admire. What is it about them that makes you love them so much? Let's explore how might you want to be more like them? Take some time to write these things down, or draw them if that is easier for you.

Someone I admire and the things I like about them:

Everyone's values can be different. And there are lots of different ways to think about these! Some of us might think it's really important to be good at school and some of us might really think it's important to play sports or music. For some of us, maybe that value would just be "doing your best".

Sometimes it's hard to know, or to name what it is you care about. And sometimes, these things can change as you grow too. This can make it harder to figure out what's actually important to you. We're going to put a menu below and we want you to put an x beside the things below that seem important to you in your life right now.

having friends	
being close with your family	
doing well in school	
doing well at sports	
having a sense of humour	
being good	
listening to parents and teachers	
being kind	
sharing	
being free	
being responsible	
being fair	

telling the truth	
doing the right thing	
doing things by myself	
not giving up when things get hard	
being religious	
being spiritual	
being brave	
standing up for my friends	
being curious	
being adventurous	

Or, you can choose your own!

Just a few notes on the stuff that you care about. Firstly, the things that you chose above are not right or wrong and some of these things might feel right for you right now, but they could change next week.

what's the answer?

1+1=

What we mean by that is that sometimes, maybe during the school year, you care a lot about doing your best at school. Maybe in the summer, you care more about spending time with your friends or going on adventures or just relaxing. None of those things are right or wrong. None of them are bad values. Human beings just often care about different things at different times in their lives.

Also, you might sometimes have noticed that it's really hard to name what you care about because maybe you have lost a lot of things and it hurts to even think about it. Maybe you care a lot about being a good friend but you can't visit your friends because your parents won't let you out. Maybe this means that you really care about getting to make your own decisions or be more in charge of your own life and your own time. Or sometimes someone does or says something really unfair and you get really angry. This might mean that fairness or justice is something that you really care about. The reason you get angry or upset sometimes is because maybe other people or situations seem like they are getting in the way of you doing more of the stuff you care about.

How do you actually do the stuff that matters when it seems like there are so many things in the way??

This is kind of like following a compass to bring you in the right direction. Sometimes you're heading in the right direction but a big storm comes and blows you off course. Let's imagine you're heading north and you look down at your compass and you realise that,

"Whoops, you're actually heading west!", you could just point yourself north and change direction. That's the great thing about using the stuff you care about as a compass. What you care about, or your values, can always guide you in the right direction.

Of course, it's one thing to discover what you care about – your values – and it can be a whole other story to actually act on them! How do you think you are doing right now at acting on your values? We know it's not always easy.

Let me give you an example from my own life. When I was little, I remember my parents always talking about how important it was to be kind. And I agreed with them because I liked when my siblings and other kids were kind to me. But sometimes I was tired or cranky and my little brother annoyed me and I'd tell him to "shut up" or "go away". This didn't bring me *towards* my value of being kind. It brought me away from it. If I wanted to move *towards* being kind, what do you think I could have done? Maybe used nicer words to let my brother know that I needed some space?

I think all of us probably have some examples of when we didn't move towards the type of person we wanted to be. All human beings make mistakes. Of course, it's easy for our threat detectors to pick up on that information *after* something has happened. And it's easy for me now, as an adult, to just say that I probably shouldn't have said mean things to my brother. If I wanted to act towards being kind, I could maybe even invite my brother to play with me. But you don't always think of these things in those moments when you're stuck.

Can you think of a time when you acted in a way that moved you *towards* what was important to you? Tell us about that or draw a picture of it in the box below.

What was that like? Wouldn't it be great if it always looked like that?

What might that look like for you? What is the stuff that matters for you? Does it include you doing well at school? Does it mean getting along with your family? Does it mean feeling safe in your home? Having good friends? Or maybe learning how to play the piano? Maybe it involves inviting the new kid over to your house at the weekend? Or maybe it means getting involved in a community project to increase recycling efforts in the area? We think all that stuff is important too. But what would it look like and feel like to *you*?

Let's use your imagination again for a few minutes. Either have someone you trust read this next section to you, or listen to Dr. Sarah's recording, or just read it over by yourself and then close your eyes and try to complete the exercise in your mind.

Audio track

www.pavpub.com/tired-of-anxiety-resources

Take a few good, deep breaths, even close your eyes if that feels ok for you, and settle into your chair again.

Now we want you to think about those things that are *really* important to you. What are those things? You don't have to say them out loud, unless you want to, but really try to settle on some things that are important to you.

And now we want you to choose an action that brings you closer to one of those things. So if you chose learning to play the piano, maybe this looks like asking a parent to get you some lessons, then going to the lessons, then learning a complicated series of notes and then being on stage performing in front of a big audience! Wow! That sounds exciting!

Or maybe it involves doing something really fun with one of your good friends or your cousin maybe. And maybe this would look like you making a plan and talking to one of your parents and your friends or cousins about how to make it actually happen. But think about what it would be for *you*. Picture it.

Let's take a few moments to really imagine this. Really picture each and every detail. See those details clearly in your mind, like you're watching it all happen. Like, you're on the sidelines of a really good game, and

you're seeing it all happen right now. Or maybe you're in there, actually doing it. Living and breathing in every single second of this, as it happens. What are you wearing? Who's sitting beside you? Look around. What can you smell? What can you see? What does it feel like to be doing this thing that is so important in your life? I bet it feels pretty good, right? Breathe in every second of it. See if you can commit this to your memory as though it's happening right now. And remember, this is your imagination, so it can look however you want it to. Oh that *is* nice, right?

Then slowly let those images fade away and open up your eyes and have a good stretch, if that feels right to you, and come back fully to this room, to this moment, with us again.

Now take a moment to write down what you imagined.

Sometimes it's hard to think about and move closer to the things you value because hard stuff gets in the way. You might value adventure, but you're scared to get lost! You might value being brave but when you think about speaking up, you feel really anxious and your voice starts to shake and then you get embarrassed about your shaky voice so instead you stay quiet. And then, when you don't speak up, you feel sad and annoyed and not good enough, and the more you feel sad and annoyed and not good enough, the less likely you are to speak up. Doesn't seem like this is going to bring you to the places that you really care about, does it?

 # Home practice

This week, we'd like you to think about the stuff you really care about. Some of that stuff will be what you wrote down earlier in this chapter and some will be the stuff from your imagination when we asked you to close your eyes and imagine you doing what seems most important to you. The next thing we want you to notice is the things that get in the way of you doing more of the stuff you care about. You can write some notes in the section below. Again, this is a noticing exercise, but this time we're also asking you to write down the stuff you care about and what gets in the way of you doing more of that stuff. Once you have a clearer idea of what gets in the way, you will have more information and more choices about how you go forward or what you do next.

The stuff I care about	The stuff that gets in the way of me doing what I care about

6:

Building a better compass

A deeper dive into what is important and valuable to you in your life

In the last section we talked about values and how you move towards them, and you used your imagination to really get into what it feels like to act in a way that brings you closer to what is important to you. Of course, this is just a book and we are just talking about and imagining these things. Often in your real life it doesn't always look exactly like it does in your imagination. The truth is, sometimes it's really hard to always behave exactly how you want to in the world! Can you think of a time when you acted in a way that brought you away from what was important? Tell us about that too. We won't be shocked at all. We promise.

Let us tell you why. We think it's really important to be kind and to be patient, but sometimes when we might come home from work and maybe we're tired, we could ask our kids to set the table for dinner or do their homework and they might not always do what we ask. Then we might lose our tempers and forget to be kind and forget to be patient. That doesn't mean that being kind and patient isn't important to us. Those things are still super important to us. But when we're feeling tired and frustrated, we might not always *act* like those things are important to us. In fact, sometimes our actions might bring us away from what's important to us. In those moments when we're tired and frustrated, we might forget ourselves and act in a way that is both unkind and impatient because it can be really hard to remember what's most important to us when we're having a hard time ourselves. Does this make sense to you? We've often made mistakes ourselves. It's just what humans do. In the box below, write or draw about a time when you acted *away* from what was important to you.

Let's imagine that you really value being brave, but sometimes being anxious gets in the way of you doing the brave things. Maybe you really want to make friends with the new kid at school or maybe you *are* the new kid at school! If you want to make a new friend, but you're really afraid to ask a person to play with you, is that acting towards what is important to you?? Or maybe you really want to play well at football but you get a pain in your tummy every single time the ball even comes near you! How are you going towards being a good athlete or improving your physical fitness??

Let's use your imagination again, but this time let's imagine you're watching yourself in a tough moment and it's like you're observing yourself on a movie screen or a TV show where you are the main character and you see that main character moving away from what is important to them. If you were able to notice that you weren't quite acting the way you wish you could, is there something you could do, in that moment, to change the script? What could you say or do that might change things to help the main character (you) act *towards* what is important for you? Imagine there are two versions of you.

83

One is the director of this movie or TV show and one is the main character watching yourself or observing yourself moving away from what is important. Now imagine that the director (you), walks over to the main character (also you) at the side of the movie set/TV set and gives the main character some advice on how you are playing the role. What would the director advise you to do to make this movie/TV scene end the way you might want it to end? Can your character do that thing?

I bet it can! Now let's imagine you changing up that script and acting towards what is important to you?

How would that look? How would that feel? Take a few moments to notice the difference between what it feels like to act towards the stuff you care about versus how it might have felt when you moved away from the stuff you care about. Can you tell us anything you noticed in the box below?

Toward and away moves

Finally, let's make a list of the actions you might take (or the moves) that might bring you towards what is important to you and let's make a list of actions that bring you away from what is important to you?

Does this sound too easy to you? Too hard? Somewhere in the middle? What does it feel like to you? Taking it apart like this?

Let's stop for a moment and be curious. Pause.

Let's check in with you. We bet there are lots of people telling you what to do every single day. Parents, teachers, maybe brothers and sisters, maybe cousins, aunts, uncles, grandparents, maybe coaches. But right now, this is just about you. What is the stuff that is important to *you*? What might it be like to take some actions that brought you closer to the stuff that is really important to you? Is it possible? We think it is.

You see, when you have anxiety (and lots of us have anxiety), it can be hard to make the moves that bring you closer to what's important to us. We've just laid it out and talked through it all and drawn some pictures and done some exercises in our imagination, but *what is it actually like for you*? Let's do some noticing here together. Have someone you trust read the next section to you, or listen to Dr. Sarah's recording, or read it quietly to yourself and then follow along in your mind.

Audio track

www.pavpub.com/tired-of-anxiety-resources

Let's use your imagination again and see if you can notice what it might be like to hit your pause button. Go ahead, hit your pause button.

Close over your eyes. Settle in to somewhere comfortable. Sit upright but not overly rigid. Breathe in and out a few times.

And let's start by noticing your breathing, noticing yourself in the chair as you start to look at this stuff that might feel pretty scary right now.

So stepping back. Slowing it down. Breathing.

So we've talked a lot here, and you're still here. And we're still here. We think that's amazing. How does it feel to you? So let's slow it all down, and rewind, watch it again.

This is you. It's all of you. And we think it's all good. It's just exactly how it's supposed to be, just right here, right now, because you're still here. We've poked and we prodded and asked and you've answered and we've poked and we prodded and you wrote and you drew and you listened and then you did it all again, and you're still here.

Notice that. Breathe it in. Again and again.

You're still here. Just where you're supposed to be. Isn't that amazing? That's the power of you. We think that's a little bit magical. To be right here, right now, in this moment, with you.

So let's take a few moments right now to settle into you, right where you are. Do you notice anything different right now? Because we've talked a lot about things that might be hard for you right now. And yet you're still here. We love that about you. That you're still here. You've made it this far. Nice job. Congratulations. You are doing an extraordinary job of being you. And we think you are utterly amazing.

Breathe that in.

The magic of you.

Again and again and again.

Taking it all in.

Just how amazing that is, that you are still here.

As hard as this has been, you are still here. And when you're ready, slowly you can start to notice this chair that's still holding you, the ground that's still below you, smells or sounds in the room around you, and then finally open up your eyes, have a stretch and come back fully to right now. Just as you are, exactly as you are supposed to be. Isn't that nice? To be exactly where you are supposed to be.

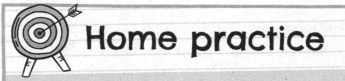

Home practice

This week, we'd like you to do some more noticing. When you notice yourself making a choice about how to act, ask yourself, does this bring you closer to the stuff that matters to you or does it take you farther away from the stuff that matters to you? If it's bringing you closer to the things and ways of being that are important to you, then great, keep it up. But if it starts taking you farther away from what is important to you, I wonder if there is something that could be done differently? What do you think? If there is some different thing that might help you re-adjust your compass and walk in the direction of the you you'd like to be, can you do that thing? What do you think? Write down what you notice in the space below.

Letting go of the fight with anxiety

Do you want to hear something strange? The more you fight with your anxiety, the less likely you're going to be able to squash it down, hide it or make it disappear. And when you do things that you care about, that is often when uncomfortable feelings like anxiety show up. It's like this brick wall just shows up in the middle of the road. What you've always done in the past – and what you're probably really good at by now – is avoiding that brick wall of difficult things and uncomfortable feelings. But of course by now, you have probably also discovered that avoidance doesn't actually work. We know. And we think that sucks too. But it's true. You might remember that we talked about this already in Chapter 3 but we're going to take a deeper dive now.

What do you think would happen if you stopped trying to squash anxiety or really any difficult thoughts and feelings down, stopped trying to pretend that giant brick wall just wasn't there, stopped trying to make it be something different? What if instead you got on your curious scientist hat (or glasses or white coat or whatever it is that curious scientists wear –

maybe they just wear normal clothes too) and what if you leaned in and looked at your anxiety a little closer? In Chapter 1 we asked you to write or draw what your anxiety looked like. If you drew it again, now, would it be different this time? Does it have a voice? Does it have a shape? Have you given it a name?

Really, all of this difficult stuff is just your mind telling you what to do at any given moment. And don't forget, our mind is pretty bossy too. Remember our mind, 'Frank'? And Frank is pretty old and pretty mean some of the time and he says lots of unhelpful things, like YOU ARE NOT GOOD ENOUGH! YOU ARE SOOOO STUPID! I CAN'T BELIEVE YOU SAID THAT! THERE YOU GO AGAIN, MAKING A FOOL OF YOURSELF WHILE EVERYONE IS WATCHING YOU!!

And we must admit that when Frank talks to us like that, it hurts and tends to make us more anxious. And it's kinda hard to ignore Frank because he's so loud sometimes. But sometimes he's funny too. There are even times when Frank makes us laugh. So what exactly do you think would happen if we just let Frank be there? What would that be like? "Oh, what's that Frank? You think I've gained weight? Why thanks, Frank. It's so nice of you to notice". Ha, I bet that's not what Frank expected! Or what if I said, "Oh hi Frank, I didn't notice you there at first. What's that you say? You think I didn't study hard enough for my test? Hmm, maybe you're right. I guess we'll find out after English class, won't we?!", or "Oh Frank, it's so nice of you to care so much. It is actually really important to me to do well at school. I guess that's probably why you're so loud and giving me soooo much advice right now. Cheers Frank, appreciate that, but I think I've got this one." Or "Hey, pipe down, Frank. Don't you know I'm trying to take a test? Shhhh! Jeez Frank, don't you know I need to concentrate right now?"

What do you think about that? Can you give your anxious mind a name too? What will you call it? Will it be a person? Or a thing? Or a cloud? Or a shadow? Maybe it's different every single time. That's also fine. Because of course, your mind is not always anxious. Our mind is lots of things depending on what is happening on any given day and in any given moment. But notice what happens when we just let our anxious minds just be here. What most people notice is that it tends not to affect us quite so much once we stop fighting with it and just let it tag along for the ride.

Write or draw what your anxiety looks like in the box below. Give your anxiety a name too and label it in the box below. Notice if your anxiety is starting to feel a little different from how it might have felt when we first started talking about it in the first chapter? In fact, after you do this section, you could look back to those early chapters and see if your anxiety is starting to feel a little different.

My Anxiety Mk. 2: What I'd call it:

_____

Let us tell you a little bit more about your anxiety. You see, when your anxiety pops up, it usually pops up because there is something there that is important to you. You probably wouldn't be anxious if the thing didn't matter. What if your anxiety was like a parent worrying that you better put your coat on because you don't want to get cold? Or what if it kept telling you to put sunscreen on so that you don't get burned? That sounds like something a parent or an older person who cares about you might do, right? Or maybe your anxiety is more like a pesky little sister who really wants to tag along but you're kind of tired of them tagging along even though you really do love them.

Is this starting to feel a little different? Do you think you could start to let your anxiety come along for the journey? I mean I had two little brothers growing up and while I thought they were super annoying when they were little, I realized over time that I really loved them a lot and in fact, now I love when they are here! They make me laugh so hard because they were with me for a lot of my life so they know me better than most people in the world. Now, I'm not saying you're ever going to beg your anxiety to come along for every journey, but maybe if you looked at our anxiety from a different angle, it might not feel quite so big and difficult?

I mean, is big always difficult? Is difficult always big?

Maybe, maybe not. What do you think?

What do you think about that?

Let's do a little more noticing together now.

See if you can notice what your anxiety is telling you now. If you are comfortable doing so, close over your eyes and have your parent read this next section to you. Or listen to Dr. Sarah's recording. Or, if you are reading this book alone, just read over the next section and after you've read it, close your eyes and see if you can quietly ask yourself some of the questions.

Audio track

www.pavpub.com/tired-of-anxiety-resources

Close over your eyes, get into a comfortable position. And when you're ready, let's imagine that you're going about the daily business of school or sport, whatever you do on any given day. And while you're doing it, you realise that your anxiety has decided to come along for the journey, and you say, "Oh, there you are anxiety. I didn't realise you were coming today." What is it telling you? Listen for a moment. It might just be giving you some information about what's important to you. What is it saying?

What does it feel like when we just let it be here? "Oh, hey Frank, thanks for coming. Actually I'm ok today, but thanks for showing me you care." Or "Oh I didn't realise you were here today Frank. What is it you think I need today? Hmmm, interesting. Maybe you're right, you could have a point there, Frank.

Do you think you could be with your anxiety like that? What would that feel like? Can you spend a few moments allowing it to be here? What if we softened up the edges around our anxiety? What would that be like? See if you can imagine your anxiety now, and see if you can imagine it getting softer, and less sharp. And maybe more like a puppy or a little kid. What would that be like for you?

Take a moment to notice what your anxiety feels like now. And when you're ready, slowly open up your eyes again and come back to the book.

You see, you don't have to love your anxiety, you don't even have to like your anxiety, but the truth is, anxiety is a part of life. I know, I know, you thought we were going to help you magically disappear all that anxiety! Sorry! The truth is, anxiety is probably coming along for the journey, but like our pesky little siblings or a cute but silly puppy that keeps eating your slippers, anxiety grows up too. And as you grow, we hope you'll start to realise that your anxious brain is just trying to keep you safe or trying to remind you to stay on alert so that bad things don't happen. But sometimes our anxious brains are like that pesky little sibling or a puppy that just hasn't yet learned that slippers aren't for chewing (unless you like that kinda thing, in which case that's your own business and we won't judge you ☺. They're your slippers.) I wonder what a difference it might make if you thought of your anxiety more like that?

Other things you can do when Frank comes to town – defusion

Defusion. You might be asking yourself, what the heck is that?

You see, when your mind gets noisy and you're feeling anxious and you're doing that time travel thing where your mind thinks of every enormous mistake you've ever made (which probably wasn't that enormous but we tend to listen to Frank a lot when we're anxious or overwhelmed or tired) and you're projecting that onto the future and saying, "Oh my God, Frank, if I fail this particular test then I'll probably fail every test FOREVER and everyone will hate me!", you'd probably listen to Frank because he is very loud and knows us very well and is really good at getting our attention.

But what if we paused for a second and slowed it all down (like we did during our mindfulness practices) and just noticed what our mind was telling us? "Frank, did you just say that I was going to be a failure forever and everyone would hate me? Ouch Frank, that hurts." And when it hurts like that, it's easy to get wrapped up in it because being successful and loved by others is really important to us. How can we stop those words from hurting us? Well, again, let's pause. Do you remember the saying, "Sticks and stones may break my bones but words will never hurt me"? Well, it turns out that words do actually hurt, but *only if we believe them*. What if you didn't believe them?

If I said to you right now, "Osioso blossom blossom, moohah, hey", would that hurt you? Probably not. Why not? Because that sentence is nonsense. We made it up. It doesn't mean anything at all. So when you read that sentence, you probably wondered what we were talking about and maybe you wondered if someone had accidentally typed a bunch of rubbish here instead of real words. Or if autocorrect was set to a different language or maybe if we were just completely bonkers, and that your parents or teachers, or whoever bought you this book, should really get a grip.

What if we when we noticed our mind saying stuff we paused and decided what to listen to and what not to listen to? Sometimes it is useful to listen to what our minds tell us and sometimes it is not. So if I'm taking a test and my mind tells me that the capital of Ireland is Dublin and that's exactly what the teacher has asked me for, then that's useful. But if I'm looking at that same test and I can't think of Dublin, and instead my mind tells me that I'm such a fool and I should have studied harder yesterday and not played video games all day when I was supposed to be studying and now I'm going to be in huge trouble? Well, that may or may not be true, but beating myself up is certainly not going to help me on this test right now, is it?

You see words can only hurt us if we respond to them as though they were cold hard facts. Many of them aren't. What if you responded to those words as though they were clouds passing by in the sky or cars passing by on the road?

As the clouds pass, you might notice that you're having the thought that it might rain or that maybe this might be a sunny day after all. Maybe if you prefer rain (like, if you're a gardener or a farmer and you need some rain), or if you want to go swimming at the beach and it would be nicer to do that on a sunny day, then this would be important. But mostly, what's happening in the sky is just what's happening in the sky. It's like background music. Maybe you like it and maybe you don't, and maybe it might suit some things and not others.

And when cars pass, you might notice that one is black and one is blue, or if you're really into cars you might notice the precise make and model, but you probably won't get into each and every single one and drive it to Timbuktu and back. There just isn't time for that, even if it were legal or possible, which it probably isn't, so far as we know.

So let's practice that idea for a few minutes. Can you close your eyes for a few moments? Like we did in previous chapters, either have someone you trust read this to you, listen to the recording or read it quietly and then do the activity by yourself.

Audio track

Close over your eyes again once more, and get comfortable in your chair, and take a few deep breaths in and out. And see if you can imagine the sky right now and also imagine that in the sky you can see some clouds. And every time a thought pops into your head, see if you can imagine that you are placing a thought onto one of the clouds in the sky.

Now, depending on the weather, it might seem that some clouds move quickly away and some hang overhead for ages, and all of that is ok. But each time a thought occurs, put it on a cloud and let it go.

Now we also want you to know that some of your thoughts, probably especially the anxious ones if you're reading this book, might come up again and again and again. And there might be other times when your mind starts to go to a completely different place, like, I wonder if we're having chicken for dinner again tonight? That's also ok. Minds do funny things sometimes.

And just like sometimes there are lots of clouds in the sky and sometimes there are only a few, whatever the weather is like, the sky is big enough to hold all of the clouds and all of the rain and all of the sunshine. And you are big enough to hold all of your thoughts, even your anxious ones. Do you believe us?

What would it mean to you if that were true? That you are big enough to hold all of your experiences?

That no thought would break you, that no thought could be too big or too difficult or too scary, because they're just thoughts passing. Just passing by at whatever speed they pass by at, on a particular day. Just another cloud in the sky. What would it be like to believe that this is true? That you are big enough and strong enough to hold all of your experiences, even the really difficult ones.

Imagine that for a few moments.

And then slowly, and when you're ready, let the images of clouds and skies fade away and open up your eyes and have a good stretch.

When we did that exercise, what did you notice? Were there some thoughts that popped up again and again? What was it like to just notice those thoughts and put them on a cloud and watch them go away? Were there times when your mind forgot what you were doing? Or were there times when you had trouble letting go of certain thoughts? Or maybe you found you liked some

of the thoughts and you wanted to hang on to them.
You probably noticed all kinds of things. Well done
to you. You did great noticing. And now, so that we
remember this for the next time, write down or draw
what you noticed in the box below.

Exercise notes: Cloud thoughts

If you found that you struggled to imagine the clouds in the sky for any reason, try this exercise instead. Or do it as well, if you have the time, and then you can compare the two later, if you like.

As always, close your eyes and get someone you trust to read this to you, or listen to the recording, or read it quietly to yourself and then do the exercise.

Audio track
www.pavpub.com/tired-of-anxiety-resources

Close over your eyes and take a few nice deep breaths.

Then, start by imagining that we are on the banks of a stream somewhere. Can you picture that? Plant your behind firmly on the banks of a stream and imagine that there's a tree overhead.

Imagine that it's September, or October, and that the leaves are starting to change colour and fall off the trees. Imagine that you're feeling quite anxious, and your mind just keeps throwing out thoughts about some disaster looming ahead.

Can you stop and listen for a few minutes? What is your mind saying?

Now, each time your mind gives you a thought, can you place it on a falling leaf, watch that leaf on the stream and watch it float away? Can you try that? Just like we did with clouds in the sky. Now, you are placing every thought that comes into your head onto a leaf on the stream.

So some thoughts might come up again and again. Some might seem to come out of nowhere. Some of our thoughts might be *really* random, and lots of them might be connected to the stuff that's important to you or the stuff that you worry about. Sometimes the thoughts and the leaves might be moving at a lightning-fast pace. Sometimes they might just sit there looking back at you for ages.

And whatever happens is ok. This isn't an effort to get rid of your thoughts. It's just an effort to notice that they are there. And also to give you a little space from them. Your thoughts are just thoughts. They may or may not be true, but if you believe every single one of them, they can be quite unhelpful. Giving yourself a little bit of space from them can help to make decisions and move towards the stuff that really matters to us.

So let's sit here now for a few more moments on the banks of this imaginary stream, and every time a thought comes up, place it on a leaf and watch it go. Stay here for five minutes or so doing just that. And if you notice your mind wandering to other places, that's ok, just place the thought that your mind was wandering to on a leaf too. And watch that go. Again, and again, with every thought that crops up.

And if you notice that somehow you seem to be in the stream fighting with a particular thought, just notice that you're doing that, gently pull yourself back up on to the bank, settle yourself back down into a comfortable position on the bank and go back to putting your thoughts onto the leaves again.

And you can stay here for a little longer if you like. In fact you can stay as long as you like. Just watching your thoughts go. And after a while, slowly let go of the images of the stream and the banks and the leaves and the trees and the flow of it all. And then slowly bring your attention back to the room that you're sitting in right now. And have a good stretch and a good yawn if that feels right for your body right now.

Nice job.

In the box below, write what your experience was like. What would it be like for you if instead of believing every anxious thought your mind had, you stepped back from it and observed it? What would it be like if your anxious thoughts didn't have so much power over you all the time? Like, they could be there but you got to decide whether or not to listen or how much you listened, or maybe that you were going to do something else altogether. Or maybe you don't do anything with them at all. Maybe you just notice that they are there, like clouds in a sky or leaves on a stream or cars passing on the road. Might be nice, huh?

Exercise notes: Leaves on a stream

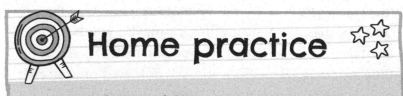

Home practice

As practice, do one of these exercises a couple of times by yourself or with your parent reading the script.

More **practice** at **step**ping back from **you**r anxiety

Have you ever had a day or week or month or hour where your head was completely full of worry thoughts – like bees in a hive? Buzz buzz buzz, whirring around, too fast for you to stop them?

Us too.

Sometimes it's hard to slow them down fast enough to even catch what the worries are! And you might just notice your body being really anxious and tense and stressed.

What do you usually do when that happens?

Try not to think about it?

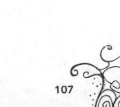

Try to push those buzzy thoughts out of your mind?

Try to talk yourself out of being so worried?

Us too! That's a normal thing to do, isn't it? When you don't like something, you try to get rid of it. Like if a bee was chasing you, you might run away.

And you know what? It works pretty well with bees! After all, you are not a flower! And you are probably big and scary to the bees – even though they might seem buzzy and stingy and scary to you!

But how does it work to run away from your thoughts? Hmm.

Let's play a game. If an adult is reading this with you, you can play it with them. The goal of the game is really simple! The first person who stops thinking about the thing we say next in our book is the winner! Let's try it. Ready?

Ok. Here's what to do: think of your favourite chocolate bar. See if you can picture it in your mind, maybe imagine holding it in your hand or unwrapping it. See if you can smell it.

Now – here's the fun part – imagine what it tastes like if you take a big bite. Mmmmmm. Yummy!

Take a moment to have fun with this. Maybe talk with your grown up about it too. Is their favourite chocolate the same as yours?

Now, STOP THINKING ABOUT IT.

Make sure there is no evidence of that chocolate bar anywhere in your mind. GO. First one who is done thinking about it wins.

So, how's it going? Is it gone yet?

How can you tell?

Are you thinking about something else? What's that?

And how do you know it's the right thing to think about? Because it's not a…

Uh-oh. There it is. That pesky chocolate bar again.

You might have just discovered a little problem: in order to not think about something, you have to keep it in your mind so that you can tell if you're not thinking about it.

Get it? Every time you check to see if you're not thinking about that thing… you think about the thing!

Turns out, there's no way to run away from thoughts in your head.

It just doesn't work the same way that running away from bees works.

There's no running.

There's no hiding.

There's no talking yourself out of them.

There's no pushing them down into a little box.

This is a pretty rotten state of affairs, isn't it?

So, now what?

Well, the first thing to know is… thoughts aren't bees.

I mean, you can think about bees. You could imagine a bee right now.

Can that bee in your mind sting you? Right here, right now?

Nope.

It's a thought. Well, it's a thought-bee.

What about your chocolate bar?

Can you actually take a bite of it now? Or share it with your grown up?

Nope.

It's a chocolate thought bar.

So if you can't eat a chocolate thought, and thought-bees can't hurt you, what does that mean?

Maybe, just maybe, there's no need to run away from your thoughts. First of all, as you have discovered, it doesn't work very well. Second of all, thoughts are just that. Thoughts.

They might be scary. Or uncomfortable. Or come with horrible feelings in your body.

And you might not like them or want them. Or you might wish they wouldn't hang around so much. Or surprise you when they pop in.

But guess what? We don't get to choose the thoughts in our head. We know. That is really annoying. But also it's the truth. Remember trying not to think about your sweet? Yup. We didn't get very far with that.

We are not in control of our thoughts any more than we are in control of the weather. Rainstorms just blow in sometimes. And then the sun comes out. It just happens.

Just like the thoughts in our head just happen.

Here's the good news! There is something you can do when your head is full of buzzy, worry thoughts.

And it works better than trying to run from them. And trying to push them down. And trying to argue with them. And trying to fight with them.

Know what it is? The best way to learn it is to try it out! This is something you and your grown up can do together too!

The first step is to see if you can slow your thoughts down so you can notice what they are. Take a few nice, deep, long breaths, sit back, and take a peek and what your worry thoughts are. Take five minutes and see how many you can write down here (or you can ask your grown up to write them down for you. They can write theirs down, too!) When you write them down, start each one with "I'm having the thought that…" You could even make it a contest – see who can notice more thoughts – you or your grown up! (We think you will win!)

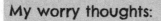

My worry thoughts:

When you are done, take a moment to talk with your grown up. Ask them what they notice when they wrote down their thoughts. Ask what they felt in their hearts and in their bodies. Then, see if you can notice your own feelings and body. What was it like to not run away from your thoughts, but instead, to notice them, and label them?

Look at them right there on the page. Look at the squiggly lines that make up the letters in each word of your thought. Look at the spaces between the words. Notice what colour ink or pencil or marker or crayon the words are in. See how many letters make up one of your thoughts.

Now, take a moment, and think about those scary thoughts when you first started reading this chapter. Compare how you were feeling about them then – when you were running away from them – to now – when you spent some time playing with them, noticing them, and choosing to be curious about them.

Did some of those worry thoughts lose their sting? Maybe even just a little bit?

You are just starting to learn some different things that you can do when your head is humming with buzzy worry thoughts. You can:

- label them
- notice them
- write them down
- draw them
- talk about them
- play with them
- name them silly names
- sing them

What do all those things you can do about your worry thoughts have in common?

None of them involve running away from your thoughts. All of them involve:

- slowing down
- noticing what they are
- labeling them as thoughts
- letting them come and go as they please

This new skill you are learning will take some practice. Sometimes it helps to practice with non-worry thoughts and to label them out loud, and then to practice with worry thoughts.

Keep trying this out, and ask your grown up to practice, too! Be curious about how it will work as you go through your day.

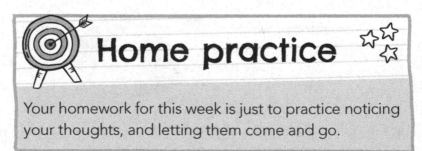

Home practice

Your homework for this week is just to practice noticing your thoughts, and letting them come and go.

10:

You are the place that your thoughts come from

By now, you are probably beginning to see that your anxious mind gives you lots of thoughts about doom and gloom because it wants to keep you safe. It doesn't want you racing head first into a disaster zone every day. The trouble is, while your mind is pretty amazing at doing lots of things, it tends to pay a little too much attention to the possibility of doom and gloom. Instead of that keeping you safe, it is most likely keeping you trapped. Ironically, while your mind might be trying hard to keep you safe, it is often getting in the way of you doing the things that are most important to you. The good news is that by giving yourself a little space from your thoughts, you can observe what information your mind and body are telling you and you can make more informed decisions about how to go forward in your life.

Do us a quick favour. Write down all your biggest worry thoughts and all the things you are afraid of for the next five minutes. Have someone time you. Ready? Go. Or if your writing isn't that great, have someone you trust set a timer and tell them all your biggest worries for the next five minutes and they can write them down.

Things I'm afraid of!

Now, we want you to pick up this book and place the part of the page with all your worry thoughts and fears right in front of your face. Right where the worry thoughts are, actually pretty much stuck to your face. Now, tell me what you can see in the room.

What's that? You could see nothing at all? Interesting. That's because all you can see are your own worries and fears.

Ok, let's take your book and hold it with both hands as far away from your face as you can. That's it. Keep holding it out there, arms outstretched. Keep it there for a few minutes. Set a timer for three minutes or have your grown up count to 180 seconds.

When the time is up, write in the space below what you noticed.

We'd be willing to bet that while you weren't blinded by your worry thoughts and fears, that the effort of holding them away from you probably started to hurt your arms after a while. So let's do one more thing with this. Let's put this book with your worry thoughts and fears down gently on your lap. What do you notice now?

We're guessing that it was a bit of a relief to put this book down because most of us find if we are trying hard to hold our difficult thoughts and feelings away from us that we get exhausted from the effort. So how about we just let them be here, sitting in our lap. We're not trying to squash them. We're not trying to push them away. We're not trying to pretend they're not there. We're just letting them be, right here where they are, in our laps. Doesn't that feel much better? Just letting it be. Interesting, isn't it?

You see, a lot of what we've been trying to tell you in this book is that you are not just your thoughts or feelings. In a way, you are the place where your thoughts and feelings come from, and sure, your thoughts and feelings are part of you, but they are not everything. You are so much bigger and more spacious than just one big fear or one big difficult thought. You are the sky. You are the stream. You are already everything you need to be.

Would you be willing to close your eyes again and try another mindfulness piece? You can have a parent read it to you, or you can listen to the recording, or you can read it first and then close your eyes and do the practice yourself.

Audio track

www.pavpub.com/tired-of-anxiety-resources

Close over your eyes again and settle yourself into a comfortable and supportive seat. Hold your body upright, but not overly rigid. Notice any particular sensations or thoughts that might be trying to get your attention right now. And gently nod your head to them, and then set them aside for the next while.

Now, notice your breathing: in and out, in and out. Notice the rhythm. Notice if your breathing is smooth or jagged. Notice the rise and fall of your chest as you breathe. There's no need to change anything. Just observe what's happening right now. And settle into you.

Now I want you to use your imagination again. And I want you to imagine that you can see a younger you, doing 'younger you' things. Maybe you can see your first day of pre-school. Maybe you were scared. Maybe you were really excited about all the toys and the new friends. Maybe you were terrified about your parents leaving you there.

Whatever it was for you, I just want you to see yourself there. Really go there in your mind; try to remember everything you can. Was there a particular smell? Or can you remember what you were wearing? Or can you remember, for example, if you fell and somebody

caught you? Can you remember who you sat beside or who you played with?

Spend a few moments going through all the details of the 'you' that was there on that day. Really breathe it in as though it were happening now, as though you could watch it happening again, from the place you are sitting right now. Try to take it all in, as though everything you needed to know was right there in those moments.

And now I want you to imagine that those images just fall away, just like somebody has changed the channel on your television. The television goes all fuzzy and the next thing a different picture comes up on screen. Of course, this is still your imagination, but we are guiding you through.

Let's take an image of you going to school now. What might you be wearing on any given day? Can you see yourself putting on a uniform or whatever clothes you usually wear to school? Can you see yourself going to school? How do you get there? Do you walk? Do you take a bus? Or maybe somebody drives you? And what do you see along the way to school? Does anyone come with you? A brother, a sister maybe? A neighbour, cousin? And can you see yourself arriving at the school?

What does your school building look like? Can you picture it now as I'm asking about it? All the details are important, just like they were important when you were in pre-school, though it might seem like

a slightly different 'you' that's observing it now.
Of course, you're slightly older, maybe you look
different, maybe there are different children sitting
beside you and I bet your teacher's different too.
And maybe your hair is longer? Maybe your feet are
bigger. Lots of things have probably changed.

But there are things here that are still the same too,
right? Maybe you still have the same brothers and
sisters, or perhaps you've gotten some new ones
since? Maybe some other details have changed. But
maybe you still like to be outside or maybe you still
like music, or maybe you're still a kid that enjoys the
summers best. So whatever's true for you right now,
I want you to take that all in, all the thoughts and
sensations and feels; and all the details of everything
that matters right now. Your hopes, your thoughts,
your dreams. All of it.

I want you to breathe it in with all of you.

Now I want you to do one more thing. But first, let
the images of this current 'right now you' just fade
away. I want you to imagine that you're looking at a
person from a bit of a distance, and you're thinking
this person looks a bit familiar. It takes a while for you
to figure it out, but finally you do.

This person is 'future you'. This is the you that
you'll be in ten years' time. Where do you think you
might be? If you could imagine that you were doing
something you'd love to be doing in ten years' time,

what do you imagine it might be? Would you still have the same friends, or might they be completely different? Do you think you'll still be in school? Or depending on how old you'll be in ten years, do you think you'll have a job? Imagine all those details.

See 'future you' in all the details you can possibly imagine, every little thing. What do you think your hopes and dreams will be about in ten years' time? What will take up your time and your energy? What will your life be about? Can you breathe that in, with all of you? Every ounce of every detail of 'future you' is yours. Breathe it in, like it matters, because it does.

'Future you' knows all the parts of you. 'Future you' knows all the versions of you at all the ages and stages. Now, if 'future you' could give 'current you' one little piece of advice, what might it be? What would 'future you' tell 'current you'? See if you can listen really carefully, and hear what 'future you' has to say to you.

Then slowly let those images fade away, and when you're ready slowly open your eyes, and if it feels right for your body right now, have a good stretch.

Write about this exercise in the space provided below. You can also draw a picture or have someone help you with the writing if you wish.

Exercise notes: Past and future you

You see, there are lots of versions of you. I'm sure your parents probably remember clearly the day you were born, though I'm also sure that you don't remember that day! But you were there then too. You brought that version of you all the way to pre-school and while it was probably bigger than the newborn version of you and maybe had more hair and probably could walk and talk, it was still you. And you are the you that sits here right now, reading this book or maybe having someone read it to you. And there will be lots of pieces of you that carry through to future versions of yourself because even though we might look different as we get older and we might have different friends and teachers and interests, we are still the same person that has observed all of our life's experiences along the way. And there are many more adventures still to be had.

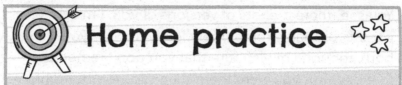

Home practice

Write or draw about some adventures you'd like for 'future you' to have.

11:

Really **going** after **you**r an**xie**ty

Now that you have learned all the skills about facing your anxiety and practiced them, it might be time to take this all a step further and *really* go after it!

What do we mean by that? Well, think about this example. Let's say Frank has been telling you a story that he is going to rob your house! And you have spent lots of time locking doors, and even though Frank might be outside lurking, you are not going to let him push you around. So you go about your business inside, and Frank still talks to you through your window, telling you he'll find a way to break in. And you keep doing what you are doing. And even though he's talking to you, he has no power over you.

But one day you decide, you know what, I'm going to *go after* Frank and *really* show him that no matter what he says he's going to do, it doesn't matter to me. So you decide to open your door and let him in. And first, you are really scared and worried that he's going to rob you! But then you notice something – Frank is a big bluffer! He's good at stories, but he often doesn't do what he says he will! So you start *going after* Frank! You leave

your wallet in front of him! And your laptop! And all
your favourite things, so he could steal them. And you
might say, "Go on, Frank, why don't you steal my stuff? I
dare ya!" And Frank, for all his bluster, sits there looking
sheepish and small. And the more you prod and poke
at him, the more you learn that Frank is an awful big liar,
and maybe he doesn't even deserve your attention!

So if you decide to really go after your anxiety, what
might that look like? Here are some ideas for you!

- If you are scared to go into a room without your
  parents – find the scariest room in the house and
  visit it!

- If you are worried about trying a new food, take a
  giant big bite of it!

- If you are afraid to try a new thing, do it anyway –
  and seek out new things to try – just to push back
  on your anxiety!

- If you feel weird sitting on a chair that might be
  contaminated or dirty, sit your bum right down
  on that chair, and your hands, and legs, and even
  your face!

First, your anxiety will yell at you – it will *hate* that you
are doing these things! But then it will learn that it
cannot push you around – that you are brave, and that
you will keep winning these battles!

It's ok to ask your parents for help to do these really
hard things. You need a team! A squad! A posse!
A platoon who can support you as you go on attack.

And even though sometimes it's hard to ask for help, it's so important if you really want to go after your anxiety.

There are lots of things you can do to go after your anxiety. If you picked some really big things, what might they be? Draw a picture of them here. And in your picture, draw the people who you want to help you face the things that worry you.

Ways to go after my anxiety:

12:

Nobody's perfect!

Wow, you are still here! You made it! We're nearly all the way to the end of the book! That. Is. Amazing! Give yourself a big pat on the back for doing the hard work. You are amazing!

You might be worried that you didn't learn all the stuff in our book perfectly, or you didn't practice it all the time, or you had some hard days or even weeks or months when you gave in to your anxiety.

We know. And that's a normal, expectable part of learning how to face your fears. Nobody's perfect! Not even your parents! Not even us – we all mess up and forget to be brave sometimes. And that's ok. Once we notice it, we can do something about it.

Sometimes when we feel like we didn't do stuff properly or well enough, we can be pretty hard on ourselves. Have you ever noticed how your mind talks to you if it thinks you didn't do a good job at something? Sometimes our minds can be harder on us than anyone else.

When you haven't done something as well as you'd like, or you feel like other people expected of you, have you ever had thoughts like:

- I'm just not good enough

- I'll never get it right

- There's something wrong with me

- I just can't do it

- It's just too hard

- Everyone will be disappointed

- I'm so bad at this

- What's the point, anyway?

If you do, you're not alone. Our minds work like that too. In fact, *everyone's* minds work like that. Do you remember our chapter where we talked about your mind (or your anxiety) being a threat detector? Sometimes part of the threat detection it does is making sure you feel bad about stuff you didn't do well. It does this so that if you feel bad enough maybe you'll work harder next time.

But that doesn't work too well for us. Does it work well for you? It just kind of makes us feel sad and bad. What about you? You see, even though your mind is a threat detector, it's not always helpful in how it tries to keep us safe. Sometimes – like when it goes negative like this – it isn't helpful at all. And we're not saying that your mind has to be positive all the time. It doesn't. Some days have bad things in them and it would be unusual if we didn't notice that or if we pretended that made us happy. The important thing to remember here is that you are not alone if you feel this way.

So what do you do when this happens, when your mind talks to you like this? You can teach it a new way of talking to you!

Imagine that you have a coach or a teacher who is really kind to you. How might that person talk with you if you made a mistake, or if you didn't do so well at something? Here are some examples:

✔ Next time you'll do it better.

✔ Good work trying!

✔ It's ok to try again tomorrow!

✔ Nobody's perfect!

✔ You're doing the best you can!

✔ Be gentle with yourself!

✔ Everybody has hard days!

✔ It's ok to ask for help!

✔ I believe in you. I really, really do.

✔ You've got this.

Write down some of the things a kind coach or
teacher might say to you here.

The skill you are learning here is called self-kindness. It just means being kind to yourself and while that sounds really obvious, it takes some practice to get into the habit of being kind to ourselves. Sometimes it's harder to be kind to yourself than others, so you can practice saying kind things to people in your family – siblings, your parents, aunties and uncles, grandparents, cousins. Try it out and see how that works. And don't forget to try yourself too! You might notice that speaking to yourself kindly is more helpful than speaking to yourself in a critical way.

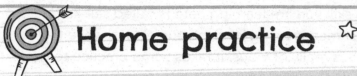

Home practice

During the week, see if you can notice when your mind – your threat detector – is speaking to you unkindly. See if you can say something to yourself that is kind and encouraging. Write down here some of the things you noticed your mind saying, as well as the kind things you practice saying to yourself when you feel like you don't get things right. It's a great idea to ask your parents for help with this, too!

Things my mind says	Kind things I say to myself

Commitment – Saying yes and meaning it

We started out this book talking about anxiety and how anxiety can get a good hold of your collar and sometimes it feels like there is nothing you can do to break free of it. But it turns out that your anxious mind and thoughts only have a big hold on you if you believe everything they tell you. And you don't have to do that.

If you step back from your mind and think about what is important to you, you get to choose how you live your life. And yes, of course, there are tons of tricky and difficult things that happen along the way, but you've already got everything you need to live the life you want to live.

What's the catch, you say? Well, living the life you dreamed of for the future versions of you might sometimes mean making some changes. Lots of people who feel anxious wait until they stop feeling anxious before they start living the lives they dream of. Unfortunately, it usually doesn't work that way. Usually, you start to feel courageous by doing the stuff you're afraid of. As a smart lady called Brene Brown says, "You get to courage by couraging".

Let's think of some examples from your life. Fill in the box below with some things that you'd like to do in the next year.

Now we're sure you know that if you want to run a marathon, and the most you've ever run is three miles, you're not going to go out there and run a marathon tomorrow. If you want to run a marathon, you're going to have to train every day. In other words, you're going to have to DO something. Your anxious mind might say, "What's that you say, couch potato? You think you can run ten miles?" Yes, actually, Frank, I believe I could do that. But let's think about what our actions might need to look like in order for that to happen. So if you want to do something brave, like sleep on your own when you've always slept with your parents, you may want to work your way up to that by practicing. What other actions might you need to take in order to get the life that you'd like in the future, or even the life you'd like next week?

Now we know that this isn't always going to be easy, but we think you've got what it takes to have the life you want. In fact, we think you always had it, but we're really pleased that you brought us on your journey.

In the box below, we want you to write your top tips for reminding yourself anytime you forget that you've already got what it takes. What might 'Next Week You' need to remember to do courageous things? What might 'Next Week You' need to remember when Frank gets too loud and forgets that he's supposed to be helping you on your journey and not preventing you from doing the stuff you love?

My Top Tips:

Finally, let's do one more mindfulness piece. Like we said already, we believe you've already got everything you need to do brave things and face your fears. Furthermore, we know that everyone has fears and most people face most of their fears along the way. And interestingly, the more willing you are to open yourself up to this difficult and scary stuff, and to look at it with curiosity, the easier it is. Now, that was a strange plot twist!

Audio Track:

www.pavpub.com/tired-of-anxiety-resources

Close over your eyes, and get yourself comfortable in your chair again. And now I'd love if you could imagine yourself feeling free. Imagine that Frank is still there because after all, he's part of you too (and you might need him someday when your brother tells you to jump off a high dive and you haven't yet learned to swim!) but imagine we don't need to get rid of him after all.

What would it mean to be free?

What would that look like?

What sorts of things might you need to do to get there? Yes, we know (we know!) that it might sometimes be hard, but let's really imagine you knowing what you need to do and doing it, again and again and again.

Because you've braved this storm and you will brave so many more. Breathe in to that, to all the 'yous'. You've got this. We believe in you. Breathe in and breathe out. And notice your chest rising and falling. Notice the places in your body that touch the chair. And notice the chair that holds you. Notice the floor beneath you supporting you, and your chair holding you.

Notice that you've done this, all of this, and that you can do it again as many times as you need to.

We believe in you.

And what would it be like if from this moment forth, you believed in you too? Say to yourself some small phrase that you might wish a coach or a loving friend or a parent or a grandparent could say to you in a difficult moment, and hear those words again and again. Let them wash over you. Breathe them into all the parts of you. You've got this.

Every time.

Every single time.

Now open your eyes and have a fresh look at this marvellous world that's just waiting for you.

SARAH CASSIDY, PHD, has worked as a psychologist in private practice in Ireland for twenty years, specialising in the assessment and treatment of emotional, behavioural, mental health, neurodevelopmental and learning differences in children and adolescents. She is Founder and Director at the Smithsfield Clinic and Co-founder and Co-Director of the New England Centre for OCD and Anxiety, Ireland Branch. She also lectures and researches in Psychology at Maynooth University. She is a Peer Reviewed Trainer in Acceptance and Commitment Therapy, a member of the Association for Child and Adolescent Mental Health, and a Chartered Member and a Council Member of the Psychological Society of Ireland. Finally, she is a Member of the Division of Clinical Child and Adolescent Psychologists of the American Psychological Association.

LISA W. COYNE, PHD, is Founder and Senior Clinical Consultant of the McLean OCD Institute for Children and Adolescents, and Assistant Professor in the Department of Psychiatry at Harvard Medical School in Boston, Massachusetts, USA. She also founded and directs the New England Center for OCD and Anxiety. She is co-author of *The Joy of Parenting* (with Amy Murrell), *Stuff That's Loud* (with Ben Sedley), *Acceptance and Commitment Therapy: The Clinician's Guide for Supporting Parents* (with Koa Whittingham), and *Stop Avoiding Stuff* (with Matt Boone and Jennifer Gregg).